CHARLES DICKENS

Charles Dickens was born in Portsmouth in 1812. He studied at Wellington House Academy and worked as a law clerk, court stenographer and shorthand reporter, which led to his first collection of pieces, *Sketches by Boz* (1836).

His major works include *The Pickwick Papers* (1836), *Oliver Twist* (1837–9), *Nicholas Nickleby* (1838–9), *A Christmas Carol* (1843), *Martin Chuzzlewit* (1843–4), *David Copperfield* (1849–50), *Bleak House* (1852–3), *Hard Times* (1854), *Little Dorrit* (1855–7), *A Tale of Two Cities* (1859), *Great Expectations* (1860–1), *Our Mutual Friend* (1864–5) and the unfinished *The Mystery of Edwin Drood* (1870), as well as other novels, books and short stories. None of his major works has ever gone out of print.

Dickens married Catherine Hogarth in 1836 and had ten children with her. He died in June 1870 from a stroke and, contrary to his wish to be buried in Rochester Cathedral, was buried in Poet's Corner of Westminster Abbey.

HUGH JANES

Hugh Janes was an actor for over twenty years, making his stage debut aged ten. He has since written over forty plays, musicals and site-specific pieces, as well as television and films. He was a writer and script consultant on the BBC series *Play Away* and devised *Scatterbox* for ITV. Other television includes *Beyond the Wall*, *Conversations with a Stranger*, the series *Second Time Around* (BBC), and the film *Even Break* (BK Films).

Stage plays include *After Dark* (Bikeshed Theatre), *Master Forger*, *Two of a Kind*, *The Perfect Murder* (from a story by Jeffrey Archer), *Deadlock*, *Dancers* (Mayfair Theatre), *A Soldier's Song* (from the book by Ken Lukowiak), *The Complete Ring of the Nibelung (abridged)*, the 'Ring' cycle in eighty minutes with all the jokes Wagner left out, *Dangerous to Know* (from the book by Barbara Taylor Bradford), *Land of Lies* (co-written with Gerald Moon), *Sealed Knot*, *Four Quarters* and *Downtown Dash*, *Ophelia* and *Museum of Horror* (at the Edinburgh Fringe in 2011), and *Riot in The Royal Oak*.

Two of a Kind, *Deadlock* and *The Perfect Murder* are published by Samuel French and were produced by Bill Kenwright.

Hugh was Writer-in-Residence for the Barbican Theatre and Plymouth Libraries, and wrote many shows for them including *Janners, Time & Tide* (also filmed for ITV) and *Divine Darkness* (YOTA Award). As Artistic Associate of Part Exchange Theatre Company he has written *The Last King of Devonport* and *Guildhall Tours*.

His feature film *Wide Blue Yonder* starring Brian Cox, Lauren Bacall and James Fox, directed by Robert Young, premiered in 2010.

Hugh Janes

THE HAUNTING

Adapted from ghost stories by
Charles Dickens

NICK HERN BOOKS
London
www.nickhernbooks.co.uk

A Nick Hern Book

The Haunting first published in Great Britain as a paperback original in 2011 by Nick Hern Books Limited, The Glasshouse, 49a Goldhawk Road, London W12 8QP

Reprinted 2012

The Haunting copyright © 2011 Hugh Janes

Hugh Janes has asserted his right to be identified as the author of this work

Front cover image by Tim Everett, Target Live; courtesy of Bill Kenwright Limited
Cover design by Ned Hoste, 2H

Typeset by Nick Hern Books, London
Printed and bound in Great Britain by Mimeo Ltd, Huntingdon, Cambridgeshire PE29 6XX

A CIP catalogue record for this book is available from the British Library

ISBN 978 1 84842 215 5

Production Notes
Hugh Janes

Bill Kenwright commissioned this play for production at the
Theatre Royal, Windsor, followed by a national tour. These
notes are based on that original production and the creative
ideas behind it.

Adapting from Charles Dickens

Charles Dickens wrote some of the most popular novels in the
English language. The richness of his characters, narrative
descriptions, his concern for social reform, his comedy and his
strong storylines mean his work is continually being adapted
into one medium or the other. When I came to write *The
Haunting*, I thought all Dickens' ghost stories had probably
been done too – but no.

I already had the basic idea for the story; one of my uncles was
an antiquarian book dealer in Brighton and, during a visit to an
old Sussex manor, he was looking at some books in the cellar
when a woman appeared. She watched him for a while and then
vanished; he knew she was a ghost. He returned to the manor on
several occasions, hoping to find out more about her, and it was
written about in the local press, but the woman never
reappeared. Although my uncle's story was a start, I needed
more and fortunately came across some of Dickens' short ghost
stories, which appeared either as independent pieces, or were
included as part of a novel.

Individually the tales didn't strike me as dramatic enough for
the stage, so *The Haunting* is a blend of five short stories with
elements of Dickens' private life, his books and letters. The fog
that creeps off the river crept straight out of *Bleak House* and
the short ghost tales *The Queer Chair* and *A Madman's*

Manuscript both appeared in *The Pickwick Papers* (1837). *The Haunted House* came out under its own name in the Christmas 1859 issue of *All the Year Round*. *The Ghost in the Bride's Chamber* is taken from *The Lazy Tour of Two Idle Apprentices*, which itself appeared in *Household Words* in 1857, which he edited. *The Haunted Man and the Ghost's Bargain* was published in 1848 and ends with the words 'Lord, keep my memory green.'

Many aspects of *The Haunting*, especially the character of David, are based on Dickens himself. He was a great reader and a solitary walker. When he worked on *A Christmas Carol*, which he called 'this ghostly little tale', he 'never left home before the owls went out' and 'walked about the streets of London, fifteen and twenty miles, many a night when all the sober folks had gone to bed'.

Dickens was fascinated by spiritualism and often visited mediums. Even after he learned the nature of their gimmickry he continued to visit. He loved trickery and was a proficient magician himself. He describes how he and a friend entertained a large gathering of children at Christmas with 'wonderful conjuring tricks. A plum pudding was produced from an empty saucepan, held over a blazing fire kindled in Stanfield's hat without damage to the lining.'

Dickens' wife, Catherine, had a young sister Mary, who doted on him, and when she was sixteen went to live with the family. One evening they all returned home from the theatre and Mary went up to bed. Moments later she uttered a terrible choking cry and died the following day. She was seventeen. Dickens took a ring from her finger and wore it for the rest of his life. His deep feelings for her were displayed in a letter to Mary's mother. 'After she died I dreamed of her… sometimes as a spirit, sometimes as a living creature… I never lay down at night without the hope of the visitor coming back to me in one shape or other.' My inspiration for the character of Mary came from this revelation.

The Ghost and Effects

What cannot be seen is often more terrifying than what can, and this is certainly true in *The Haunting*. The bride is not frightening when clearly lit and is a much more effective apparition when glimpsed briefly. For those few times she is onstage, she should be a shadowy, spectral figure who appears suddenly.

The first time she is seen is in a lightning flash, and in this case she should be brilliantly lit but for a very short time. The sightlines of the French windows should not prevent any member of the audience seeing the ghost in the tree.

The use of light and sound are important elements in a play that sets out to scare an audience. Darkness, shadows and flickering half-light, prevalent in the days before electric light in the home, are an asset here. The less we see of the ghost and the greater use that is made of what might be lurking in the gloom, the better the chances of startling the audience. Raising the volume of a sound cue is enough to cause an audience to jump. It is important to create an atmosphere of the unexpected, and the noises around the house and the character's uncertainty about what is happening all add to this mood. Some eerie music can also be used at the start and in scene breaks to good effect.

Set and Design

The play is set *c*.1865 and the costumes should reflect this period and the social positions of the characters.

The house in which the study is set is from a much earlier period and described as 'the obsolete whim of a forgotten architect'. The original production's set benefited from numerous angles and period features that facilitated the ghost's appearances – she was never seen 'coming on', but was suddenly in the room.

Although a lot of books are required, there is no need to fill the bookshelves with real ones. A run of false spines was quicker for stage management to remove in scene breaks, as if David had taken them down for cataloguing and packing.

The idea for the set came partly from a description in *The Haunted Man* and partly from an engraving by artist Robert Buss, which shows Dickens sleeping in a chair in his study surrounded by the spirits of his characters and books. A photograph of the same room and an illustration called 'The Empty Chair' by Sir Samuel Fildes, who illustrated *The Mystery of Edwin Drood*, provided complementary elements.

Furniture and fittings can be any period prior to 1865, but the Victorian style seems to suit the mood of the play perfectly.

Thanks

I would like to thank Bill Kenwright, Josh Andrews, Tim Welton and Hugh Wooldridge for their help in bringing the original production to life.

The Haunting was first performed at the Theatre Royal,
Windsor, on 2 November 2010, before touring the UK, with the
following cast:

LORD GRAY	Paul Nicholas
DAVID FILDE	Sean Maguire
MARY	Hannah Steele
Director	Hugh Wooldridge
Designer	Simon Scullion
Costume Designer	Jonathan Lipman
Lighting Designer	Nick Richings
Sound Designer	Jonathan Suffolk
Original Music	Laura Tisdall
Producer	Bill Kenwright

The Haunting was revived at the Theatre Royal, Windsor, on
7 February 2011, before touring the UK, with the following
changes to the cast:

DAVID FILDE	Charlie Clements
MARY	Emily Altneu

Characters

DAVID FILDE, *a book dealer, mid-twenties*
LORD GRAY, *a middle-aged businessman*
MARY, *a young bride*

ACT ONE

The study of an ancient manor house.

Books and objets d'art fill the dusty shelves. On one side is a large fireplace with shelves either side. A door leads to an antechamber (off). Opposite, a door leads to a corridor and the rest of the house. A bare tree is seen outside the French windows, upstage centre. It is night: the wind howls.

A lamp flickers beyond the window. Horses whinny, their hooves resound in a courtyard as they turn and draw a carriage and the light away. DAVID, asleep in a wing chair, wakes with a start, pulls his coat back round him and returns to sleep. A distant door creaks and slams. Footsteps echo along the corridor, then stop outside.

LORD GRAY *enters with an oil lamp and looks about before seeing DAVID.*

GRAY. There you are, young man.

DAVID *wakes and stands, shivering.*

DAVID. Lord Gray? Forgive me, sir. I fell asleep.

GRAY. So it seems. Are you cold?

DAVID. I'm freezing, sir.

GRAY. Someone of your age shouldn't feel a slight chill.

DAVID. It was snowing outside when I arrived.

GRAY. A peculiarity of this part of the moor.

DAVID. No, in the hall.

GRAY. Ah, that will be the tiles, or lack of them.

DAVID. Is that why it feels colder inside than out?

GRAY. Quite possibly. I've seen icicles at that window in the spring. External temperatures have little influence on me.

DAVID. You are fortunate, sir. This is a considerable change to London.

GRAY. That will be the fog.

DAVID. I didn't see any fog.

GRAY. You won't in these parts, but I understand it covers London like a blanket.

DAVID. It creeps off the river and festoons its entrails about everything.

GRAY. Filthy stuff.

DAVID. I almost miss it.

DAVID *'warms' himself by the unlit fire*.

GRAY. You'll get more warmth from a pea-souper than you will from that hearth. It hasn't seen a fire in years.

DAVID. It's enough to see the flames in my mind's eye. (*Looks about.*) This room is full of strange fascination. I can tell great minds have been at work in here.

GRAY. Can you? My lawyer only recently received word of your firm's change; I take it you've letters of recommendation?

DAVID. Would you care to see them now?

GRAY. Tomorrow will be no good if they're unsatisfactory. You're so late I'd quite given up on you.

DAVID *hands letters to* GRAY *to read*.

DAVID. I'm sorry for it, sir, but there was a terrible incident as we were driving away from the station; a woman threw herself into the path of the carriage. She panicked the horses and was kicked by one of them. It happened so quickly there was nothing your driver could do to prevent it.

GRAY. She was probably staggering from The Railway Tavern.

DAVID. Even so, I insisted on taking her to a doctor. She said she only tried to stop the carriage to warn me not to come here, though how she knew it to be my destination I cannot guess.

GRAY. Word travels easily in a small community.

DAVID. She kept saying, 'I know the secret of the tree.' Does that mean anything to you?

GRAY. Why would her ramblings mean anything to me?

DAVID. She claimed to have worked here.

GRAY. Perhaps she did when the estate was thriving. The farm manager may have known her.

DAVID. Her name's Edith Renwick and she'd been a servant.

GRAY. Then the housekeeper would have dealt with her.

DAVID. Does it not seem extraordinary?

GRAY. Only your fixation with something of complete indifference to me. We've both been inconvenienced by this woman; now let it be an end to the matter.

DAVID. Forgive me, the episode was after a long and tiring journey.

GRAY. You're clearly unused to country ways.

DAVID. It's true, I have not travelled far outside the metropolis.

GRAY. These appear satisfactory.

DAVID. Then allow me to present the firm's new card.

> DAVID *takes a card from his pocket and proudly hands it to* GRAY *to read.*

GRAY. 'By Royal Appointment'?

DAVID. To His Royal Highness the Prince of Wales, and the monarchs of two countries. Filde has been a trusted name for nearly one hundred years.

GRAY. 'Edward Filde and Nephew, Dealers in Antiquarian Books, Manuscripts and Engravings.' You, I take it, are 'and Nephew'.

DAVID. Yes, sir.

GRAY. How long have you held this position?

DAVID. I have been a nephew all my life, sir.

GRAY. Within the company, Mr Filde.

DAVID. My uncle took me as apprentice when I was twelve, after the death of my mother. I was promoted to partner this year and my designation added at the last printing. It is a great honour.

GRAY. Your father is not part of the firm?

DAVID. Sadly he passed away two days before my mother.

GRAY. You were fortunate to find a benefactor of good character.

DAVID. My uncle is the finest humanitarian, the ablest teacher and the kindest man. He has offered me the greatest of opportunities, as he did for my young sister.

GRAY. That may be, but he was not averse to passing my business to someone only recently advanced.

DAVID. He taught me most diligently.

GRAY. I expected him to show a more personal interest in the valuing of this collection. Your firm was only chosen because of the relationship he had developed with my father over many years.

DAVID. He talks of it often and was upset to learn of Lord Gray's death. He sends his condolences.

GRAY. Please thank him for them.

DAVID. I will, my lord. In fact, he knew this estate would be of particular interest to me.

GRAY. Oh, and why is that?

DAVID. For a number of reasons. Also, my uncle rarely travels
outside London now. The bookshop takes up more hours
than he likes. Although, he still attends the London sales and
his opinion is sought on all matters by the trade.

GRAY. Even so…

DAVID. When he was young he despatched a special edition of
Dante's *Inferno* to Napoleon himself when Bonaparte was in
exile. The transaction required extreme secrecy, for fear of
spies using it to contact the Emperor with plans of espionage.

GRAY. I had no idea the book trade was so bracing.

DAVID. It is rarely as academic as one thinks. I'm making
notes for a story about my own adventures.

GRAY. It would be extremely vulgar if any of my affairs were
made public, or my privacy invaded in any way.

DAVID. I certainly wouldn't…

GRAY. Nor should fanciful notions impede your judgement.

DAVID. I can assure you, my lord, they won't.

GRAY. Very well. Now, may I offer you a glass of port wine?

DAVID. You are most kind.

GRAY. In the absence of a fire it may provide some inner
warmth.

DAVID. Indeed, sir.

GRAY *picks up the lamp.*

GRAY. Light a lamp. Don't stay in the dark in here.

GRAY *exits; as his light disappears down the corridor*
DAVID *is plunged into darkness.*

*The wind builds and a sharp scratching comes from the
window. Moonlight filters in to reveal a branch scraping the
glass.*

DAVID *lights a lamp and looks about. He takes a book from
a shelf beside the fireplace, looks at it and replaces it. As he is*

moving his hand over other books one shoots out with a noise and falls on the floor. DAVID, startled, picks up the book.

DAVID. How peculiar.

He opens it and a key falls out. DAVID retrieves the key.

'Curiouser and curiouser!'

DAVID *is pocketing the key as* GRAY *returns with the lamp and two mean glasses of port on a tray.*

GRAY. What is that?

Showing him the book.

DAVID. Er… *Crime and Punishment.* Dostoevsky. A Russian. Book-club edition – perhaps sixpence.

GRAY. Why start with the cut-price rubbish?

DAVID. It sort of came to hand.

He replaces it and GRAY *offers the drinks.*

Thank you, your lordship.

GRAY. I am not a heavy drinker but sometimes a glass or two as a nightcap helps me sleep.

DAVID. Exactly what my uncle says.

GRAY *flicks dust from a chair with his handkerchief and sits.*

GRAY. I had hoped your uncle would handle this matter, because the situation is rather delicate. My father, the late Lord Gray, left his estate in considerable debt.

DAVID. Forgive me, my lord, but this does not entirely surprise me.

GRAY. Oh?

DAVID. I'm afraid he owed Fildes nearly seven hundred guineas.

GRAY. I'd no idea. So much? Just for books?

DAVID. I have the invoices with me.

GRAY. Of course, they will be settled – in time.

DAVID. He was such a long-established customer and had, until the past few years, always paid punctually. My uncle sometimes has a rather sentimental approach to debt.

GRAY. Now I see why he sent you.

DAVID. It is one reason, yes.

GRAY. My businesses are mostly abroad so I knew nothing of my father's indulgences, but they are legion. I last saw him several years ago and settled some minor accounts I put down to oversight. To protect the family name, I must sell everything.

DAVID. I am sorry to hear that, sir.

GRAY. Most of the contents of the house have already gone. The solicitor dealt with it. I wanted to manage this room and my own apartments.

DAVID. Must you even sell the house?

GRAY. I loathe the place, nothing but expense and miles from anything resembling civilisation. It's simply the obsolete whim of a forgotten architect. Smoke-aged, weather-darkened, squeezed on all sides by that frightful moor. The sundial is in a bricked-up corner where no sun has straggled for a hundred years, but where, in compensation, the snow will lie for weeks when it has lain nowhere else.

DAVID. It's difficult to ignore its solitude. As the carriage approached the house in the gathering dusk it appeared to impose itself over the landscape like a blackened shroud.

GRAY. Well, young man, you certainly could write fiction.

DAVID. My inventive faculty sometimes runs away with me.

GRAY. Indeed. Now, there is much to do and little time to achieve it. My return passage to India is already booked.

DAVID. Is the entire collection here?

GRAY. Yes. The remainder of the house will be of no interest to you.

The wind, which had abated, builds again.

DAVID. On the contrary, my lord. I study the architecture of old buildings. My sister lived in just such a house and her letters were highly descriptive. It would be an opportunity for some practical observation.

GRAY. You will not have time for indulgences.

DAVID. Of course, sir.

GRAY. I consider literature as nothing but the buttress of pedantry. However, I need to realise the highest price for mine and am counting on your expertise to guide me to it. I will not be fobbed off.

DAVID. No, sir.

GRAY. No one was allowed in here. It was my father's inner sanctum. He was meticulous and couldn't abide others meddling with his things.

DAVID. I've encountered gentlemen of a similar disposition.

GRAY. He kept his world secret.

DAVID. The secrets will be in the words.

GRAY. I've never liked this study, but something about it obsessed my father. You'll sleep in here.

GRAY *opens the door to the anteroom (off)*. DAVID *follows and looks in.*

My father used this antechamber when he was working. He died in that very bed.

DAVID. Thank you. It looks most comfortable.

GRAY. You'll find everything for your needs. I anticipate your diligence, Mr Filde.

DAVID. You shall have it, sir. I trust you will not find me wanting in any department.

GRAY. That remains to be seen. We shall start first thing. I bid you goodnight. (*Takes a lamp.*)

DAVID. Goodnight, my lord. Lord Gray?

GRAY. Yes?

DAVID. Do you know who's purchasing the house?

GRAY. Not personally. He's a philanthropist who wants to turn it into a school for the sons of distressed gentlefolk.

GRAY *exits*. DAVID *glances about*.

DAVID. I feel sorry for the children already.

A key sounds turning the lock.

Lord Gray?

DAVID *tries the door handle. He is locked in.*

My lord? How strange.

DAVID *takes the key from his pocket and tries it in the door – it doesn't fit.*

The wind reaches a sudden crescendo. A rasping noise comes from above, like fingernails scraping a board, and grows until there is a crash in the courtyard. DAVID *calms himself and looks out of the window as the wind abates.*

A tile, nothing but a loose tile. Another snowdrift in the hall. What have I let myself in for?

He picks up the lamp and his bag, exits into the anteroom and shuts the door.

Darkness. The faint sound of a woman's voice is heard calling eerily.

MARY (*off*). Help me. Help me.

DAVID *returns with the lamp.*

DAVID. Lord Gray, is that you?

MARY (*distantly*). Please, help me.

DAVID. Who's there? Hullo, who's there?

DAVID *eases his way to the main door; it is still locked. He taps gently; silence. He looks about the room and moves nervously back towards his room.*

I think I might regret coming here.

He exits and shuts the door.

Scene Two

Next morning. Sun lights the room. DAVID *is on a library ladder; he wears cotton gloves. Books are on the desk and floor. A horse-drawn carriage is heard outside.* DAVID *looks then brings books down from a shelf and notes them in a ledger. A magpie screeches outside.* DAVID *goes up the ladder and resumes work.* LORD GRAY *enters with a tray of food and tea.*

GRAY. So, Mr Filde, busy at work already, I see.

DAVID. No period within the four-and-twenty hours is so valuable to me as the early morning.

GRAY. My sentiments entirely.

DAVID. In the summertime, I often rise early to set part of the day's work aside before breakfast.

GRAY. A sharpened appetite focuses the mind.

DAVID. I'm always impressed by the stillness and solitude around me.

GRAY. You will find nothing but around here. I've engaged a couple from the village to call once a day and perform whatever duties are necessary. Twitchin, who met you, is the only person hereabouts with a carriage. His wife will bring food so you can work without distraction.

DAVID. That's most considerate.

DAVID *anticipates being given something but* GRAY *helps himself.*

GRAY. Has your morning provided me with any significant benefit?

DAVID. Your father built a very fine library.

GRAY. I am aware of that.

DAVID. I have an inventory of all the books we supplied, most of which are still here. They will only need comparing against the current catalogue price. What first caught my eye are some of his Bibles.

GRAY. Oh?

DAVID. This, for example, is a Wycliffe manuscript.

GRAY. How much is it worth?

DAVID. Look. See the craftsmanship.

GRAY. I can come here at any time and look at books; all I want from you is their value.

DAVID. I will need to verify the price with my uncle to be…

GRAY. You assured me of your expertise, if you are wasting my time…

DAVID. Not less than two thousand pounds.

GRAY. Two thousand?

DAVID. That is a conservative figure.

GRAY. For just one book?

DAVID. This is not just any book. John Wycliffe believed that, as Christ taught people in a tongue they understood, he should do the same. He was the first to produce handwritten Bibles in English. This one is dated 1384, the year he died. It is exceptional.

GRAY. This is much more to my liking. What else have you unearthed?

DAVID (*picking up the book*). Another rare Bible.

GRAY. Splendid.

DAVID. This was printed in 1631 and is known as the King James 'Wicked Bible'. It isn't known how many survive. The printer was fined three hundred pounds and ordered to destroy all copies for omitting the word 'not' from the Ten Commandments.

Opens it and shows it to GRAY.

GRAY. 'Thou shalt steal.' I always knew it.

DAVID (*reads*). 'Thou shalt commit adultery.'

GRAY. What fun! At last a religion I can subscribe to.

DAVID (*reads*). 'Thou shalt kill.' (*Shuts the book.*) Words in books, my lord, shall reap rewards.

GRAY. Indeed, although in this case missing words can reap even more.

DAVID. I'm cataloguing as I inspect and the books fall into three categories: exceptional, such as these. Excellent, many of the scientific and medical books are unusual and will attract specialist buyers. And the remainder, which individually are worth little, will defray your costs.

GRAY. Your bill I suppose.

DAVID. Also for the sale.

GRAY. Why would that incur costs?

DAVID. Transportation. Cataloguing. Auctioneer's fee. You didn't expect me to have a banker's draft for many thousands of pounds in my pocket and simply take all of these away?

GRAY. You are book dealers?

DAVID. Precisely, we deal in books; we don't collect them ourselves.

GRAY. All I require is payment.

DAVID. It would be impossible to outlay a sum reflecting their true value. Any dealer prepared to would offer a lot less than they are worth.

GRAY. So, what do you propose?

DAVID. That we inform the collectors who will purchase the rare, specialist works through us.

GRAY. That's most unsatisfactory.

DAVID. You will achieve much higher prices.

GRAY. I will?

DAVID. We can auction the best volumes in London, where they will obtain the strongest interest. The others will do just as well sold in Braunton. To speed the process we can send details of everything to my uncle and he will notify collectors right away.

GRAY. How?

DAVID. I hoped you could have them taken by the mail each day.

DAVID *takes an open envelope from the desk and hands it to* GRAY.

May I have some food now? I've eaten nothing since yesterday and the smell of the bread and cheese is overwhelming.

GRAY. Of course.

DAVID. I am grateful, sir.

GRAY. Did the port wine help you to a good night's sleep?

DAVID. Remarkably so – following the initial surprise.

GRAY. What was that?

DAVID. After you left I heard a voice.

GRAY. A voice? Whose?

DAVID. I don't know. It was some way off, and quite faint – yet the words were distinct.

GRAY. You surprise me. The house was quite empty, apart from ourselves.

DAVID. There were no servants here?

GRAY. Not until this morning.

DAVID. I'm convinced I heard it. Faintly calling from – well, I cannot be sure from where, in here, or just outside somewhere.

GRAY. My apartments are in the north wing and I assure you I neither walk nor talk in my sleep.

DAVID. I didn't think it would be you, my lord, in any case it sounded like a young woman's voice. It must have been no more than the wind and your coachman's anxiety playing on my mind.

GRAY. Twitchin has a reputation as one who spins a good yarn. What's his latest notion?

DAVID. That the house is haunted.

GRAY. Haunted? It's not the first time his unguarded comments have caused provocation.

DAVID. When I asked what made him think it, he said, 'Well, I wouldn't spend a night there.'

GRAY. He's right. Twitchin is a simple coach driver with no chance of staying anywhere but above the stables. Don't believe his nonsense.

DAVID. He said if he wants to hear bells in the house ring, with nobody to ring them, doors in the house bang, with nobody to bang them, and feet stamp about, with no feet there, 'Then,' he said, 'I'd stay in that house.'

GRAY. Did you hear those noises last night?

DAVID. They would have scared me witless if I had.

GRAY. Your own senses did not detect the phantoms of village hallucination?

DAVID. No, but I wasn't hallucinating last night.

GRAY. So all we have are Twitchin's unreliable words and your own uncorroborative senses. I have lived in two so-called haunted houses, young man. In one of these, an old Italian palace which had been twice abandoned on that account, I

lived eight months most tranquilly and pleasantly. I heard so
many strange noises they would have chilled my blood had I
not warmed to them by dashing out to make discoveries.
There is always life in the night. Listen for it in bed in a
darkened room as a gentle breeze turns into a demon's howl.
Or look for it in the comfortable firelight when warm coals
conjure wild faces and the crackle of logs becomes the cackle
of witches. Then you can fill the house with noises until you
have a noise for every nerve in your nervous system.

DAVID. Perhaps I shouldn't have felt agitated had I not been
locked in.

GRAY. This door was not locked.

DAVID. I tried opening it, it wouldn't budge.

GRAY. You may be working here but you're also my guest; I'd
not be so impolite as to lock you in. (*Opens and closes the
door.*) Perhaps the inclement weather swelled the timbers.
Anyway, your work is in here, if you begin wandering the
halls you will end up like Twitchin, quaking at your own
inventions.

DAVID. If that's what it was.

GRAY. What other explanation is there?

DAVID. Perhaps he heard the sounds.

GRAY. And no one else did?

DAVID. He was here alone.

GRAY. Now I know he's talking gibberish.

DAVID. It was some years ago, just after your father had gone.

GRAY. Gone? Yes, he did move to London for a time.

DAVID. Fled, according to Twitchin.

GRAY. Another elaboration. I believe it was to do with his work.

DAVID. Yet he passed away here.

GRAY. Something always drew him back.

DAVID. Whatever you thought 'obsessed' him?

GRAY. Perhaps. He certainly didn't indulge in melodramatic fiction.

DAVID. I'm merely trying to piece together the mystery.

GRAY. With wild speculation. There is no mystery; he probably just wanted to die in his own house. Perhaps he was fleeing his creditors. He became a recluse; even the servants were dismissed or left because of him. But do continue with Twitchin's fantasy.

DAVID. Well, he said that while your father was in London he was asked to give a lecture at the Royal Scientific Institute.

GRAY. He was a member. What had that to do with Twitchin?

DAVID. The late Lord Gray had left a book here that was significant to his presentation and sent instructions for Twitchin to send it on.

The carriage is heard arriving and then sounds and actions continue as described and build to a frenzied crescendo.

It was dark when he arrived and let himself in. He lit a lamp out in the hall, unlocked this door and came in. The book was not where your father said he would find it and, being a man of limited literacy, it took him some time to search. He became aware of a servant's bell ringing, seemingly, in the kitchen. He looked out into the hall, wondering if in fact the house was staffed, and the ringing stopped. Twitchin returned to his search when the ringing started again, only this time it got louder and was gradually joined by all the other bells. As if all the servants in existence were being summoned together. Twitchin pulled open the door again and yelled, 'Stop them damnable bells.' And slammed the door! To his delight, the sound stopped. When he felt ready he continued his search. Only this time he heard footsteps in the room above. They creaked out along the passage and down the stairs. He heard them walk along outside in the hallway, until they reached this door. He stood spellbound as slowly the door began opening. Suddenly all the doors in the house began opening and banging together. Twitchin grabbed an entire pile of books, collected the lamp and ran out into the corridor as fast as ever he could, yelling the name of every Saint he could summon to assist him. As he ran down the passageway he heard all the footsteps in Hades racing after him, pursuing him the entire length of the corridor until he pulled back the door, threw himself out into the fresh air and charged his horses helter-skelter into the night.

Silence. The events have left them stunned.

GRAY. That was quite a tale, Mr Filde.

DAVID. Rather more than I expected. Did you hear it too?

GRAY. The ears of the deaf would have been dumbfounded.

DAVID. That was hardly the invention of a 'simple coach driver'.

GRAY. No. It was not.

The horses whinny and clatter hooves on the flagstones; GRAY *steadies himself.*

Ah! There goes your faith in Twitchin's lurid extravagance. Everything we just heard is because he and his wife are still about. I'd forgotten.

DAVID. I'm amazed they remain employed making that amount of noise. Perhaps you could ask them what they were doing.

GRAY. Horses whinny of their own free will. Doors bang through draughts. Bells ring when they are dusted. In my experience there is always an explanation for what appears inexplicable. I'm sure whatever Twitchin heard has the same logical account.

DAVID. You will allow me to keep an open mind on the matter, at least for the time being.

GRAY. As you please. Now I must see Twitchin before he leaves; I'll have him take this to the mail.

LORD GRAY *exits, shutting the door.* DAVID *opens it; content, he shuts it and works. Lights fade.*

Scene Three

Evening. The tray is gone, books piled up, and DAVID *is working in the gloom. The sound of scratching is heard near the chimney. It stops, then begins again more frantically. It is joined by a faint call.*

MARY (*off*). Help me. Help me.

Several books shoot off a high shelf above Crime and Punishment; DAVID *stares at them. Cautiously, he picks up the books.*

DAVID. Who are you? What do you want?

He looks up at a gap left by the books and stands on a piece of furniture to reach it and bring from the rear a folder. He takes out letters, documents and newspaper cuttings. He is reading a small letter when GRAY *enters.* DAVID *puts the letter in the folder and puts it aside.*

GRAY. I am not usually taken off balance, Mr Filde.

DAVID. I am pleased to hear that, my lord.

GRAY. Even here among the worm-eaten beams, and thundering echoes in the empty rooms, I remain sensible to my surroundings. Now, as nightfall releases outlandish shadows to frown out behind half-open doors, I am self-contained. It was therefore difficult to realise the game you played with my perceptions.

DAVID. I don't understand you, sir.

GRAY. I was taken by surprise and briefly succumbed to folly, but if you think you're clever enough to fool me with elaborate sounds and trick doors you're very much mistaken.

DAVID. You believe I concocted that?

GRAY. Yes, in order to startle me.

DAVID. Not only would such fabrication require the dexterity and skill of the Great Rubini, why would I do it?

GRAY. Money, Mr Filde. That is the reason this estate is, in your words, of particular interest to you.

Distant thunder rumbles, as the scene continues it gets closer and louder.

DAVID. That is not the reason; in fact you are very far from it.

GRAY. Every book is permeating your mind with its cash equivalent.

DAVID. That's preposterous, sir.

GRAY. You brought current values of everything you've supplied, assuming many would still be here. You could easily assess their value on your journey from London.

DAVID. You may search my bags and check if I have hidden volumes. How would I even bear their weight?

GRAY. With Twitchin's assistance.

DAVID. I never met the man until he brought me from the station yesterday.

GRAY. Perhaps, but you knew a coachman was meeting you, someone potentially open to bribery, and the rest is governed by circumstance.

DAVID. I am more inclined to believe this is some elaborate hoax laid on for my benefit rather than yours. Though to what end, I cannot say.

GRAY. I assure you I am not a person to instigate hoaxes. Something like this would require what I believe is termed 'theatricality' of the type commonly associated with cheap music hall or comic opera. I have been to neither.

DAVID. Sir, you must accept my innocence. My letters of recommendation are from men whose integrity is beyond reproach.

GRAY. Theirs may be; yours is not.

DAVID. Then I must leave your house at once, to prevent this stain you are spreading upon my reputation from tainting my uncle's.

GRAY. It's impossible for you to leave.

DAVID. Why?

GRAY. I sent Twitchin and his wife away with your mail. He will not return till morning.

DAVID. I shall walk, as I do in London.

GRAY. The moor is full of mires and quicksand. A city-dweller like you would perish before reaching the bounds of the estate.

DAVID. Are you to hold me prisoner?

GRAY. You cannot leave until our business is settled and we've an explanation for this charade.

DAVID. Then I must ask you not to take advantage of your position to impugn my name.

GRAY. That remains to be seen. Even if I believe you, for all I know Twitchin has some kind of grudge against me.

DAVID. For what reason?

GRAY. His inability to secure a permanent position since he left our employment.

DAVID. He could find himself more than compensated for that loss carrying the trunks of a hundred spotty schoolboys to and fro.

GRAY. Don't take me for a fool, Mr Filde. If you are meddling in my business, you will see you have picked the wrong employer.

DAVID. I would never do such a thing. I thought you dismissed the noise as draughts and domestic activity.

GRAY. Twitchin said they were going about their work as instructed and heard nothing untoward.

DAVID. Then it's even stranger that the sounds and actions were confined within the walls of this room… my lord.

GRAY. He did hear one thing.

DAVID. Oh?

GRAY. The distressed cries of his horses.

DAVID. What startled them?

GRAY. They're horses. They'll ride unflinching into a fusillade and panic at a leaf taking off in the wind.

DAVID. But did you ask him about the tale he told me yesterday?

GRAY. The hauntings and whizz-bangs in the night? Yes, he said he may have heard something about it in the village but didn't recall mentioning it to you.

DAVID. Then where would I have gathered such a fantastical story?

GRAY. If Twitchin still drinks as he used to, he'd not remember from one day to the next whom he regaled with his fairy stories. I suspect half my father's cellar was decanted down his throat straight to his imagination.

DAVID. Does extreme inventiveness besiege him when he is soused with drink?

GRAY. Who knows what comes to us in the rush of intoxication. There is another alternative.

DAVID. Which is?

GRAY. It was my father's story and during his stay in London he invited your uncle to his club and created the fabrication to impress him. The fantasy was passed on to you for your own false bells and phoney footsteps.

DAVID. I would point out I was locked in this room all last night.

GRAY. So you claim.

DAVID. Did I manufacture bells from coal scuttles and warming pans? Did I climb through secret cloisters under the foundations to hang them where they would sound most effective? Did I conjure actors to career along corridors and give voice to curses I had penned for their vocational skills?

GRAY. For all I know any of this may be true.

DAVID. Or none of it. And now you accuse me of colluding with my uncle.

GRAY. I will get to the bottom of this.

DAVID. Yet he and your father couldn't have met under those circumstances.

GRAY. How can you be so sure?

DAVID. Because my uncle was most embarrassed by their one encounter.

GRAY. Oh?

DAVID. Since their association was built over many years via the mail, my uncle didn't know what your father looked like, or indeed, the other way about.

GRAY. Naturally.

DAVID. One day he was dining with members of the Book Guild when he overheard a waiter say your father's name. Seeing him dining alone, my uncle thought the conviviality of a restaurant an ideal first meeting place. He presented himself. Your father turned ashen and said, 'I cannot speak to you here.' With that he left and we never heard from him again. My uncle was humiliated but took no slight, assuming his own breach of etiquette in approaching unannounced.

GRAY. I thought I had given up apologising for my father.

DAVID. There's no need.

GRAY. Perhaps he thought he was about to be handed your bill.

DAVID. Possibly, but the idea of their geniality is unlikely.

GRAY. I was brought up in this house and in all the years I lived here I never heard such noise or reports of any the like. If I rush to explanations it's because none rush to me.

DAVID. Supposing the truth is the most obvious thing we've overlooked.

GRAY. Which is?

DAVID. That what we saw and heard actually occurred.

GRAY. Of all the ideas that came to me, none is more unbelievable.

DAVID (*getting it*). This folder was hidden, right at the back of that shelf.

GRAY. So?

DAVID. I only found it because a number of books – hurled themselves onto the floor.

GRAY. It is unsurprising in a room veiled in stillness for years that new vibrations will shake loose a few books.

DAVID. The books were thrown.

GRAY. Are you sure they weren't bowled out in some elaborate cricketing gesture?

DAVID. You may mock me, sir, but it's what happened.

GRAY. Whenever a tale sprinkles off your tongue, effects and illusions seem to accompany it like wearisome chaperones.

DAVID. I was working here and heard the same voice I heard last night.

GRAY. Ah, the voices, the voices.

DAVID. Immediately afterwards the books leapt from the shelf.

GRAY. Well, there is your answer; they were calling for your attention. When you ignored them they prostrated themselves before you.

DAVID. I know what I saw and heard.

GRAY. Wandering through India, as I have for many years, wherever there is a market or town, I found fakirs and charlatans making people believe that inanimate objects can spring to life and move of their own volition. Children as thin as wraiths climb ropes that uncoil impossibly from baskets and rise towards the sky. The child then scurries upwards without any apparent support. It is known colloquially as the Indian rope trick.

DAVID. Unless you think I have the power of a fakir, an art I will have mastered in total ignorance of the subject, it seems there is such a thing as the inexplicable phenomenon.

GRAY. Inexplicable I grant you, but don't attempt to label it as ghostly or any other such nonsense.

DAVID. Yet your father considered it serious enough.

GRAY. What do you mean?

DAVID. Do you know a general dealer in Braunton called Gabriel Grub?

GRAY. He used to carry out maintenance duties on the estate. I didn't know he owned a shop.

DAVID. It seems your father bought it for him before he went to London.

GRAY. An act of generosity far beyond his miserly nature.

DAVID. This was in the folder.

He hands documents to GRAY.

GRAY. It's from our lawyer, confirming the purchase of the store and gifting it to Grub.

DAVID. Read the page torn from the journal.

GRAY. This is my father's writing.

DAVID. I recognised it from his correspondence.

GRAY. 'Mr Grub reported to me today he also saw the figure. He was outside the window cutting back the tree from scratching the glass, when he heard the barn owl screech its tormented sound. At that moment a young woman appeared, inside the room, hovering in the misty light. Grub turned away, thinking he was gazing at his own distorted reflection in the pane, but when he turned back he saw the figure still there – fading before his eyes.'

DAVID. The barn owl is also known as the ghost owl.

GRAY. That's foolish nonsense.

The thunder is much closer and joined by thin lightning flashes.

DAVID. Is it? Perhaps that's the secret in the tree.

GRAY. Many superstitions enjoy undeserved reputations. Foolish notions often come to resemble fact.

DAVID. Indeed, there is often nothing so plausible as unfounded gossip. But I wondered if that figure were your reason for staying away from here.

GRAY. I am hardly to be kept away by something that does not exist.

DAVID. Don't you wonder at the mystery that occurs between this existence and the next?

GRAY. Every country I visit has different beliefs. In England alone there are probably a hundred organised notions about the soul. You may believe in some condition between life and death, I do not.

The thunder and lightning are very close.

DAVID. That's very close.

GRAY. Electrical storms are not unusual here. The moor attracts such phenomena.

A bird crashes against the window, coupled with the screech of the ghost owl.

DAVID. What's that?

GRAY. Probably a bird confused by light coming from both directions.

DAVID. Have you seen it before?

GRAY. Never.

DAVID. What does it mean?

GRAY. That a bird was disorientated.

DAVID. Was it the ghost owl?

GRAY. Don't be ridiculous.

DAVID. If it were, then possibly there's some truth in Grub's story.

GRAY. If you continue in this vein I will say goodnight.

> GRAY *turns to leave and there is a flash of lightning.* DAVID *turns to the window and outside, apparently standing in the tree, is* MARY. *Her bride's dress, once cream, is now ragged and smeared with age and filth. Her frayed veil partly obscures her face, which is pale and wasted. She is staring into the room.* DAVID *is terrified. Immediately it goes dark outside again.*

DAVID. There, there. Did you see that?

GRAY. See what?

DAVID. The woman in the tree?

> *The lightning flashes again – but* MARY *is gone. The tree is empty.*

GRAY. What woman? The tree is bare.

DAVID. There was a woman there. Standing among the branches.

GRAY. A trick of the lightning forming peculiar shadows is all.

DAVID. A woman. In a ragged dress. A bride's dress.

GRAY. A woman in a bridal gown?

DAVID. Yes.

GRAY. You've had a long and tiring day and are in need of refreshment.

DAVID. Please don't go.

GRAY. I am merely going to the kitchen.

DAVID. Let me come with you.

GRAY. But, Mr Filde, it would be bad manners to neglect your mysterious phantom – you've scarcely met.

GRAY exits, leaving the door ajar.

The thunder and lightning recede. DAVID *calms himself and takes the letter from under the book.*

DAVID. 'My dearest brother, I am sorry I have not written for some months but what I have to say will come as something of a shock to you…'

There is a sound of a heavy object cracking into something and fading away. DAVID *is baffled. It is heard again coming from deep in the house; it moves closer to the room.* DAVID *edges to leave, but the door bangs shut. The lock fastens with a clank. The first sound is joined by that of a young woman, sobbing. The noises grow. The cries of the woman become terrified screams, coming from inside the room.* DAVID *is suddenly aware he is not alone. He turns, and standing in the shadows near the fireplace is* MARY.

Who are you? What do you want with me?

She extends claw-like fingers towards him in supplication and her voice rasps out.

MARY. Help me. Please help me.

DAVID *staggers away from her and tugs wildly at the door, yelling.*

DAVID. Open the door. Lord Gray, let me out. Save me, for mercy's sake, save me.

He bangs violently on the door as if trying to break through, calling out.

GRAY (*off*). Stop that noise. Stop it at once!

GRAY *throws back the door and stands in the doorway; he has a bottle of brandy.*

DAVID. Thank the Lord you're here. Thank you.

GRAY. I can hardly ignore such cacophony. What is the meaning of it?

DAVID. Look, Lord Gray. The woman is here. The bride is in the room.

GRAY *enters and* DAVID *turns to point to* MARY – *but she is long gone.*

She's gone.

GRAY. If she was ever there.

GRAY *turns to go when the faintest cry is heard from* MARY.

MARY (*off*). Please help me.

GRAY. What did you say?

DAVID. You heard that?

GRAY. I heard you speak, but not what you said.

DAVID. I said nothing.

GRAY. I distinctly heard you.

DAVID. I said – nothing.

GRAY. Who is that?

As they look apprehensively around, the wing chair slowly revolves. In it sits MARY. *She holds out a crucifix. Thunder claps and wind howls. Blackout.*

End of Act One.

ACT TWO

*The following day. The wing chair is back in position. More
books are down and* DAVID *is working. Some packing cases
are nearly full. The door is open.* GRAY *enters with a bundle of
books.*

GRAY. These are all the books left among my things.

DAVID. Could you put them over there for cataloguing?

GRAY. Among the makeweights, no doubt.

DAVID. Threepence here, sixpence there, it all adds up.

GRAY. Please ensure you miss nothing of value. Well, young
man, you're looking and sounding a good deal brighter this
morning.

DAVID. Yes. I am most grateful for allowing me to share your
apartments.

GRAY. You were in no fit state to be left alone, especially not in
here. I wasn't sure you would want to come back.

DAVID. Well, I have only two days left to finish this task and –
I had to come back.

GRAY. Brave words in the light of day, but you weren't so sure
last night.

DAVID. I cannot imagine why.

GRAY. It took two large brandies before you could even speak.

DAVID. Only two? I should have been more hesitant.

GRAY. They finally restored colour to a face that was as
bleached as any I've seen.

DAVID. It felt so cold.

GRAY. Even I noticed an uncommon drop in temperature. Also that smell – of mildew and mustiness.

DAVID. And decay. Yes. Do you think that's how the dead live?

GRAY. A contradiction in terms.

DAVID. I don't believe so any more.

GRAY. There was such a commotion I thought you were being possessed.

DAVID. That was the tormented soul of that poor young woman.

GRAY. You kept saying, 'Look at her. Look at her,' and pointing in this direction – except there was no one here.

DAVID. I was convinced you saw her too.

GRAY. Not even the merest glimpse.

DAVID. Yet the chill and the odour were unmistakable.

GRAY. Yes, most strange and irrational.

DAVID. I'm finding books behind books.

GRAY. My father considered magpies virtuous.

DAVID. His papers are unending and tucked away in the oddest of places. I'm not surprised your lawyer didn't take them.

GRAY. My lawyer?

DAVID. Doesn't he need them to conclude your father's business?

GRAY. No.

DAVID. Why ever not?

GRAY. He runs the office with only one clerk for help – and couldn't find time to come out to the house and search about.

DAVID. That sounds like a fine excuse. If he didn't come here, how did he know he'd have to search about?

GRAY. He was in possession of my father's will and everything else essential to settling the estate and saw no reason to make the journey.

DAVID. It's not because he's heard the rumour of 'village hallucinations'?

GRAY. A man trained in the law does not pay attention to wild superstitions.

DAVID. Some people think it's superstitious to avoid being superstitious.

GRAY. And there are some who believe absolute nonsense.

DAVID. I have heard that said of the law too.

GRAY. You replaced Father's chair, I see.

DAVID. I thought you'd put it back.

GRAY. I've more on my mind than furniture.

DAVID. So even you were overawed last night.

GRAY. One of the most improbable things I've ever seen.

DAVID. You don't deny seeing that then?

GRAY. Quite the contrary.

DAVID. Did you see any way I might be manipulating it?

GRAY. No, but a chair will not turn of its own free will.

DAVID. So how did it?

GRAY. That is the Indian rope trick.

DAVID. Only not performed by me.

GRAY. Admittedly, you didn't look in a state to perform sleight of hand. But I've seen religious men on Mount Ararat who whirl around and around continuously and can chant themselves into a hypnotic trance. Their frenetic activity is quite at odds with their appearance afterwards, which is utterly tranquil. What are you doing?

DAVID *searches in and around the chair.*

DAVID. I just remembered – there was a crucifix. As the chair turned, it was here. Did you pick it up?

GRAY. A crucifix? No.

DAVID. We stared at it. In her hand.

GRAY. I saw something luminous. Nothing more than reflections from the lightning.

DAVID. It was here. A real crucifix.

GRAY. Carried by your invisible spirit, I suppose.

DAVID. Presumably the woman who moved the books and slammed the doors.

GRAY. Logic, Mr Filde, I must have logic. If it were real it would still be here.

DAVID. That desperate young woman pleading for help wasn't a figment of my imagination. (*Returns to work.*)

GRAY. Rational men are more inclined to the secular than the spiritual.

DAVID. Are you one of the atheists, my lord?

GRAY. Don't sound so disapproving.

DAVID. The Bible offers all of us the chance of everlasting life.

GRAY. If it can provide it while I'm still alive, I'll accept the offer. I was wondering if you have a facility.

DAVID. Facility? For what exactly?

GRAY. To perceive the presence of the spirit. There are mystics who claim to identify with the deceased, I wondered if you are one of them.

DAVID. If I am, I'm not aware of it. Though I have had a similar experience once before.

GRAY. There.

DAVID. Several years after my father had died, I woke and saw him sitting on a seat beside my bed. I knew it couldn't really be him but, at that moment, he looked alive and well. His head was cupped in his hand, a way he often held it, so whether he was slumbering or thinking I couldn't make out. I was surprised to see him there, but not in the least startled.

I sat up to observe him more closely, and as he didn't move, I spoke to him. Rather foolishly, I asked how he was keeping. Still he made no move and just sat there. Then I became worried in case he actually was there, so I stretched out to put my hand on his shoulder...

GRAY. Only there was no such thing.

DAVID. By the time my hand reached him he was gone. This lack of physical entity reassured me of his spiritual presence.

GRAY. You see, you may possess a facility, or else what you saw was a projection of your thoughts.

DAVID. Why would I have wanted to see my father?

GRAY. To reassure yourself of his presence in the next world, or to speak of things neglected in his lifetime.

DAVID. If I have many more visions I will find myself sent to Bedlam.

GRAY. The light crafts unworldly shapes at that hour of the night and our minds are wont to play tricks upon us.

DAVID. Yet what I saw in here was a ghost.

GRAY. Ghosts are things of fiction and hearsay.

DAVID. A fiction I saw with my own eyes; a woman in a bridal gown, only shredded and pitiful, as if it had been made entirely of rags.

GRAY. Was it the same woman you saw in the tree?

DAVID. She appeared no longer than a lightning strike, but I believe it was. Why?

GRAY. It seems curious you saw the same image in two different places.

DAVID. When you said earlier not to stay in this room in the dark, is the woman what you meant?

GRAY. How could it be when I don't believe such things exist?

DAVID. Do you believe in love?

GRAY. Love?

DAVID. Yes. Do you believe there is such an emotion?

GRAY. I can't say I have experienced it myself, but its existence is well recorded.

DAVID. Then where is it?

GRAY. Carried inside.

DAVID. But what does it look like?

GRAY. Ah. Once again you try to trick me with words.

DAVID. No. I also believe love exists, even though its only visibility is in the way we show it.

GRAY. You know full well it is not the same thing.

DAVID. Not the same, no, because I can see what exists here and you cannot, but it is enough that you believe in something invisible.

GRAY. It may be the only way if we are to understand this. I can't deny there has always been an eerie feeling about this room.

DAVID. Although the sight of her terrified me, I don't believe she bore me any ill will. Rather than malevolence she seemed to need help.

GRAY. Help?

DAVID. Yes. When I heard her call, that first time, she cried out for help. When I saw her she was imploring me for something. But perhaps it was all taken out on your father.

GRAY. Why would you say that?

DAVID. Is it possible it led to madness?

GRAY. You think a – spirit could do that?

DAVID. If not the ghost then whatever caused it to be here. Your father, Twitchin, Grub, Mrs Renwick all offer some form of testimony.

GRAY. Testimony to what, is the question?

DAVID. Exactly what we need to find out. If you care to look at the inventory thus far, you will see I am ahead of matters and my work here will be completed in the time you've allowed.

GRAY. Not if this isn't resolved, it will be the only thing on both our minds.

DAVID. Precisely. However, it seems whatever haunts this room only manifests itself at night. If she has a presence in the daytime she hasn't yet made it obvious. Therefore I will have the days to work and at night we shall solve this mystery.

GRAY. We?

DAVID. Do you not want to know what may have killed your father, and why he was nearly bankrupt?

GRAY. Yes, I do.

DAVID. Can that tree support a person?

GRAY. I climbed it often as a boy.

DAVID. To spy in on your father?

GRAY. Most likely.

DAVID. I'd like to know if it's still possible. We need to find out if there is any truth in Grub's story.

GRAY. That was years ago.

DAVID. We can only piece together what we have.

GRAY. Yes, check everything before moving on to... well, something else.

DAVID. Perhaps there might be a trace left of the bride's clothes?

GRAY. A piece of torn cloth?

DAVID. Anything. Oh – is there a greenhouse here?

GRAY. There was.

DAVID. If it has any flowers would you cut some and bring them in?

GRAY. Flowers? Whatever for?

DAVID. For the living.

> GRAY *exits.* DAVID *begins going through the folder as the lights fade.*

Scene Two

The lights return and GRAY *appears outside the window and checks the tree.* DAVID *enters from the anteroom with a box, and stops as* GRAY *peers in.*

GRAY. An owl may be perfectly safe up there but a person would crack these branches.

DAVID. So whatever I saw was unlikely to be living.

GRAY. There's no trace of fabric of any kind.

DAVID. Do you have a clear view of the room?

GRAY. Close to the pane I can see you moving by the hearth.

DAVID. Then they weren't lying.

GRAY. It isn't a clear view, the old glass refracts in some way.

DAVID. So it may have distorted the woman Grub saw in here.

> DAVID *puts the box aside.* GRAY *enters with flowers.*

GRAY. We must draw our own conclusions. The greenhouse is a forlorn place now. When I was young we had flowers and fruit all year. I suspect it was the warmest place in the county. Now hardly any glass remains. Will these suffice?

DAVID. The book merely says, 'fresh flowers for life'.

GRAY. Which book?

DAVID. A journal your father was writing on spiritual matters. It's fascinating, would you like to see?

GRAY. It won't be necessary.

GRAY *gets a vase to put the flowers in.* DAVID *looks through papers.*

There are huge red flowers in my garden in India that float in a bowl when they're cut. In the evening breeze they seem to still be alive. What is that?

DAVID. A personal folder I found up there behind some novels. It appears to be a family history; with photographs, newspaper reports...

GRAY. I remember my father poring over this.

DAVID. There are collectors for this type of material. Military books and paraphernalia are most sought after.

GRAY. I thought he rid himself of this nonsense.

DAVID. A set of histories and eyewitness accounts, with personal letters, would be prized. Your family has lived here for over two hundred years. Its history is of great interest.

GRAY. Books are your business. Some things should remain secret.

DAVID. What things? How it acquired the estate, for instance?

GRAY. So you know. The house was plundered by Cromwell and gifted to my ancestors for their 'loyalty' in the Civil War. It's not part of our history of which I'm proud.

DAVID. 'To the victor belong the spoils.'

GRAY. Spoils? Look at what we gained so dishonourably. An informant said the owners were Royalists sheltering an enemy. Cromwell's men searched and found no evidence but still took everyone outside and hanged them from a tree. Death has inhabited the place ever since.

DAVID. I also found this photograph. It's of a Captain Gray, in the uniform of the 14th Hussars.

GRAY. This was my elder brother, James.

DAVID. It was with this cutting from the *London Gazette.*

GRAY. 'October the fifteenth, 1854.'

DAVID. Ten days before the Charge of the Light Brigade.

GRAY. I didn't know this had been reported.

DAVID. It seems the Russians were trying to capture our port at Balaclava and cut off supply routes. It begins with a general description of the build-up of the day's activities, with movement of troops and orders being despatched. The report continues, 'The Russians...'

GRAY. Please. (*Takes the report.*) 'The Russians, their light-blue jackets embroidered with silver lace, were advancing at an easy gallop towards the brow of the hill under cover of light cannon.'

As GRAY *continues the sound and lighting take us to the battle.*

Did you hear that noise?

DAVID. Clearly.

GRAY. Just like in Twitchin's story.

DAVID. It occurs with stories related to your family.

GRAY. Do you think it affects whatever is in this room?

DAVID. Or whoever. Are you going to stop?

GRAY. No. I have to continue. '... under cover of light cannon. The instant they came in sight, trumpets of our cavalry rang out through the valley and a glittering mass appeared in front of the British encampment. The Russians advanced down the hill at a slow canter; the first line was at least double the length of ours and nearly three times as deep. The trumpets rang through the morning air and with gathering speed, the ground flying beneath their horses' feet, the 14th Hussars led by Captains Gray and Westmorland went right at the centre of the Russian cavalry.

The Russian line swung forward each wing and threatened to annihilate them as they passed. But feinting a little to their left, the Hussars bore round to meet the Russians full on and rushed at them with a cheer that thrilled every heart that heard it. The cries of the 14th resounded through the valley as their swords flashed through the core of the Russian attack and struck terror and confusion in the enemy ranks. Then the Dragoons and the Redcoats rose up from their positions on the plateau and charged, disappearing into the midst of the shaken and quivering columns in an exhibition of valour and daring, reflecting on the best days of chivalry. There was a clash of steel before Captain Gray, a renowned rider and first-rate swordsman, wheeled his cavalrymen with irresistible force at the remnants of the first line of the enemy and drove through it, scattering enemy troops in all directions. The Russian horse fled with all speed before a force not half its strength. Cries burst from every lip and men and officers held aloft their hats and shouted and cheered with all their might.'

The sounds die away and after a moment there is a heart-rending cry from the woman's voice.

Dear God! What sound was that?

DAVID. A banshee. The spirit of a woman whose duty is to warn the family of approaching death.

GRAY. What do you mean?

DAVID.
    ''Twas the banshee's lonely wailing,
    Well I knew the voice of death,
    In the night wind slowly sailing
    O'er the bleak and gloomy heath.'

My lord, your brother was killed four days later. I found this letter to your father from Captain Westmorland, explaining the circumstances.

GRAY. I knew my brother died in battle. (*Reads.*) I've never seen this. Westmorland says it was a military action of great distinction.

DAVID. He was a brave man.

GRAY. He was also torn apart with grief.

DAVID. I don't understand.

GRAY. James wrote to me that he was in love with a young woman and had asked her to marry him. He said our father disapproved as the girl was socially inferior. He couldn't cope with any scandal. Reputation was vital to his esteem and that of the family. I answered my brother that he should marry for love.

DAVID. As the oldest, wasn't he due to inherit everything anyway?

GRAY. Very perceptive. That was the main reason I left and set myself up in business in India.

DAVID. My lord, I'm afraid I have not been entirely honest with you. When I said my sister worked in a house such as this, I should have said this very house. That is the reason I was especially interested in this estate.

GRAY. Your sister?

DAVID. Due to the relationship forged between my uncle and your father it was suggested that Mary come here to be employed and taught the requirements of an upstairs maid, so that one day she could return to London and find employment in a respectable house there. Your father cannot have foreseen the consequences of his generosity. It was my sister, Mary, your brother, James, was to marry.

GRAY. A servant, from this house?

DAVID. Mary was the prettiest girl you'd ever have seen. For years she made excellent progress and reported her life in regular letters. Then when she was eighteen the letters stopped. I wrote regularly, as usual, and even asked your late father for reports on her well-being. I heard nothing.

GRAY. I cannot believe it's the same girl.

DAVID. When you contacted us about your books it provided the perfect opportunity to find out what had happened. I found this. I was reading it when the bride appeared.

He gives GRAY *the letter from his sister. He starts to read then* MARY*'s voice takes over.*

GRAY. 'My dearest brother, I am sorry I have not written for some months but what I have to say will come as a shock to you...

MARY. '...I am with child. I know I have done a bad thing but good is to come of it for Captain James Gray, of whom I have written, has promised to marry me. He is the child's father. I know our social positions are so very different but he is a wonderful, brave man who tells me I am the most perfect girl he has ever known. His father, Lord Gray, is opposed to the marriage and threatens to cut him off and so we are to elope. I am not sure where we will go or when I will be able to write to you again in the near future, but I am delirious with happiness.'

DAVID. I kept all her letters. One she wrote exactly describes this house and room.

GRAY. Why did she not send this, perhaps the most important of all?

DAVID. Either it had been taken from her – or she didn't live to send it. She was not a woman, she was a girl with no experience of life. Seduced by your brother and promised marriage, her position in this house when he left for the Crimea must have been impossible.

GRAY. You think the spirit is that of your sister?

DAVID. Yes, and that's why I can see her and you cannot. Though her face is pale and her figure hardly moves, it is dreadful to me, as it comes from the grave.

GRAY. Why does she haunt this room and no other?

DAVID. I don't know yet. (*Produces the key.*) Do you recognise this key?

GRAY. In a house of thirty-seven rooms it could belong to any lock. Where did you find it?

DAVID. In here. (*Shows* GRAY *the book.*)

GRAY. *Crime and Punishment.* You were looking at this when you first arrived.

DAVID. You may laugh, but it jumped off the shelf right at my feet.

GRAY. There is a concealed compartment.

DAVID. Just big enough for this key.

GRAY. Where is your invention taking us now?

DAVID. I am certain whoever lives within these walls wanted me to find this, but try as I might I can find no lock to match it in here.

GRAY. Is the title significant?

DAVID. I think so. In it a man, heavily in debt, kills a woman for her money but is then tormented by his action.

GRAY. Your sister cannot have been rich.

DAVID. No, but she was going to be when she married your brother.

GRAY. As I see you will not be satisfied until you have tested every lock in the house, I suggest we search it from top to bottom.

DAVID. I thought you didn't want me to see the house.

GRAY. The circumstances have changed somewhat. So, let us make the most of the daylight and explore. The night will soon be upon us.

They exit, leaving the main door open. After a moment, the door slowly closes and behind it is MARY. *Blackout.*

Scene Three

Night. DAVID *and* GRAY, *with a lamp, enter.*

DAVID. One hundred and thirty keyholes and not even one a close fit.

GRAY. I counted one hundred and thirty-three, including the cellar cupboards.

DAVID. It is hard to believe a house has so many doors.

GRAY. Light the mantles, Mr Filde.

DAVID. Does the dark worry you too?

GRAY. Only what may be hidden within it. I have a feeling we may also need this again.

He puts down a bottle of brandy as DAVID *goes to the gas mantles over the fireplace.*

DAVID. I hoped we would find an answer.

GRAY. There is not much to find in empty rooms. For all we know, that key may have fitted an outside door, or one that no longer exists. At least your curiosity is satisfied about the rest of the house.

DAVID. If anything, it is heightened.

GRAY. Now we know there are no outside influences?

DAVID. Yes.

DAVID holds a match to the first mantle and it ignites with a 'whoosh!' They both jump. The second mantle lights quietly.

I believe everything we witnessed is directly associated with your late father. The book Twitchin collected was important to him, this chair was his favourite, and it was his son, your brother, who led the charge into battle.

GRAY. And if the girl were your sister, she was associated with him too.

DAVID. Ever since I arrived I felt someone has been signalling to me. Sending messages in the only way possible.

GRAY. For someone who is beyond the grave, you mean?

DAVID. Exactly.

GRAY *goes to* MARY*'s place.*

GRAY. Why here? This is where the apparition made her appearance?

DAVID. Yes. She stood motionless in that corner, a slight and wasted figure. The blood chills in my heart as I repeat the sight.

GRAY. You said the spirit was asking you for help. Whatever can she want? What is it, Mr Filde?

DAVID. You asked what she wants.

GRAY. Well, what of it?

DAVID. Nothing. Only not so long ago you dismissed my seeing her as a trick of the light, or a manifestation of my imagination.

MARY*'s voice echoes though the house.*

MARY (*off*). Help me. Please help me.

DAVID. There. Did you hear that?

GRAY. A strange echo of sound.

DAVID. Calling for help once more.

GRAY. How can we help her?

DAVID. By freeing her from the hell of this place. If it is my sister, then I shall not be afraid. If it is not… then, I must take my chance.

GRAY. I suppose, as the saying goes, we are in this together.

Tapping is heard inside the walls.

I've heard it said that spirits remain in places where their bodies were most unhappy.

DAVID. Whatever happened in this house happened in this very room.

A terrible cry comes from the moors.

She's here.

GRAY. What do you propose?

DAVID. To set her free. Your father was dabbling in psychical research.

He gets the box he brought in earlier.

GRAY. All that mumbo-jumbo and ectoplasm?

DAVID. I cannot promise you the ectoplasm.

GRAY. It is nothing but teapot trickery.

DAVID *takes psychical things from the box.*

DAVID. That won't be the case here. Your house isn't rigged with the effects of the medium's trade. We must attempt to tap into whatever spiritual realms are in this room. It's time to release the spirit of my dear sister.

GRAY. The cynic and the credulous, hand in hand in ignorance.

DAVID *gives* GRAY *the psychical book. He reads from it as* DAVID *lays out the objects and paraphenalia.*

'First infuse the room with heated fragrance. Cinnamon provides warmth and energy for around the room. (*Pause.*) Any number of white candles that can be divided by three.'

DAVID *gets white candles and puts them with the other things.*

Now, spices. 'The use of frankincense will expand the conscious mind and id. In most ceremonies connected with the spirit world, perfumes and fumigations play an important part.'

DAVID *sets out the frankincense*.

Now we need something familiar to the spirit.

Beat.

DAVID. My sister's last letter?

GRAY. Yes.

DAVID (*brings the letter*). Is that everything?

GRAY. The flowers. (*Gets them.*) Then we should light the candles.

DAVID *does*.

DAVID. Now what, my lord?

GRAY. We wait.

They dim the lamps and sit waiting.

How do you know she'll come?

DAVID. She's already here. Can you not feel the cold?

GRAY. And the decay.

There is an eerie, breathy cry and some papers drift off a shelf by the fireplace.

DAVID. Is that you, Mary?

MARY*'s disembodied voice is heard*.

MARY (*off*). No rest or peace.

DAVID. How can I help you?

MARY (*off*). Free me.

GRAY. Free her?

DAVID. You can hear her?

GRAY. Oh yes. Free her from where?

DAVID. Give her a Christian burial.

GRAY. She's a ghost.

MARY (*off*). Don't hurt me, sir. Please don't hurt me.

DAVID. Hush, my precious. Be peaceful.

They wait.

GRAY. Is she speaking now?

DAVID. No. But I know she can understand.

MARY *appears in the gloom and beckons her bony, claw-like finger. The men are transfixed in terror.* MARY, *in a sinister, breath-laden voice, speaks.*

MARY. Know me. Know me.

DAVID. I do know you, apparition. Why do you come to haunt us, my sister? My sweet companion.

MARY. Come to me.

A gruff, disembodied man's voice is heard.

MAN (*off*). Stay where you are.

MARY. I must go.

MAN (*off*). Take off that bridal gown, girl.

The words now stumble out in a nightmarish blur. Lights pulse and the wind starts to howl. Intermittently, MARY *is glimpsed in the shadows.*

MARY. Water. I am so thirsty.

MAN (*off*). Your marriage will blight my son's life. It will never take place.

MARY. All my skin and bones are dead now.

GRAY. Who is that?

MAN (*off*). Death is all that will stop you.

GRAY. It's my father.

MAN (*off*). You will never be his bride. Or come between me and the son who is the object of my life.

MARY. We will be married.

DAVID. Mary.

MAN (*off*). A pale-eyed girl, with no character, no purpose.

MARY. I descend halfway to hell through the bowels of the earth.

MAN (*off*). A helpless nothing.

MARY. Help me.

MAN (*off*). You will never bear my son's child.

There is a terrible bludgeoning sound accompanied by MARY*'s screams.*

DAVID. Mary!

GRAY. For God's sake, light a lamp.

DAVID. No.

GRAY. It's murder.

There is crashing, battering at the outside of the door. An indescribable phenomena. Then books cascade from the shelves beside the fireplace. It is silent.

Is it over?

DAVID. I cannot be sure.

GRAY. I tell you, I shall be pleased to see morning.

DAVID. Your father killed her.

GRAY. And her unborn child.

DAVID. I should have held her in my arms. Comforted her. I never knew anyone who trusted people the way she did.

GRAY. Look. Where the books were displaced.

DAVID *joins him at the fireplace, where the door to a priest's hole has been revealed, behind the shelves.*

DAVID. There's a door.

DAVID *takes out the key and fits it in a lock.*

It is the right size.

GRAY. Don't open it.

DAVID (*steps away with the key*). Why not?

GRAY. We have no idea what's in there.

DAVID. It's a hiding place.

GRAY. The priest's hole.

DAVID. You knew your father… [had killed her].

GRAY. Rumours. That is all.

DAVID. This is where she was. Entombed and undetected.

GRAY. I had no idea. No idea.

*GRAY exits hurriedly, shutting the main door behind him.
DAVID looks towards the priest's hole, wondering whether
to open it. He goes slowly to it. Inserts the key and prises
open the creaking door. A scream of anguished pain is
released with a burst of dusty steam and a trail of
phosphorescent light. The emanation seems to fly through a
window, shattering it in a gale of laughter. A lightning bolt
illuminates the tree.*

DAVID (*yelling after her*). Mary!

*Silence. Everything settles. DAVID reaches inside the hiding
place and brings out the crucifix.*

Her only possession.

*He slowly blows out the candles and clears the psychical
things away. He pours a large brandy and sits in the wing
chair.*

To you, my beloved sister.

*He drinks, rests back in the chair, pulls a cover over him and
closes his eyes. The lights fade. It is still. The main door
opens slowly and a man enters from the darkness beyond – it
is LORD GRAY. Only he is an older, more distinguished
man and apparently more cheerful.*

GRAY. Ah, there you are, Mr Filde.

DAVID, *startled, looks up and stands.*

DAVID. Forgive me, sir, I fell asleep.

GRAY. My dear boy, whatever are you doing in this room?

DAVID. I was asked to wait here.

GRAY. I'd no idea. You might have been here all night. However did you find your way to the house?

DAVID. Your man, Twitchin, drove me.

GRAY. Twitchin?

DAVID. He said Lord Gray asked him to show me in here.

GRAY. That is curious, as I am Lord Gray.

DAVID. And I am confused, sir.

GRAY. You must be exhausted from your journey. This is such a cold room, don't you find? The books are all here and you can start cataloguing tomorrow. First, let's get you in front of a blazing fire and we'll get some food and wine inside you.

DAVID. That sounds ideal, my lord.

They start to exit.

GRAY. We are having a small celebration. My son James has just received his commission.

DAVID. Your son?

GRAY. Yes. He's Captain James Gray now.

DAVID. My lord, may I ask, is James's brother here?

GRAY. No. My younger son is in India. He has business there. Come, your sister will be so excited to see you.

DAVID. My sister?

GRAY. What a strange young man you are. I understand it's her eighteenth birthday. The staff has prepared a little party. Isn't that Mary's gift in your hand?

DAVID *looks at the crucifix, still in his hand.*

DAVID. Oh yes, the crucifix. It's to bring her safekeeping.

GRAY. She'll be safe enough in our hands, I assure you.

GRAY *exits*. DAVID *picks up a lamp and follows. As he closes the door he looks back in.* MARY*'s voice implores distantly.*

MARY. Help me. Help me.

As the lights fade DAVID *closes the door.*

The End.